IMAGES
of England

WESTLAND

The first and the last. The Wyvern was the Royal Navy's first turbine-powered aircraft and Westland's last fixed-wing aeroplane. The 3,500 hp Eagle 22 used in the six prototypes was Rolls-Royce's most powerful, and last, piston engine. It turned Britain's first eight-blade contra-rotating propeller produced by Rotol Airscrews. Seen near Beachy Head in 1953, these Wyvern S.4s belonged to 813 Squadron, the first to operate them, then based at RNAS Ford.

IMAGES
of England

WESTLAND

Compiled by
Derek N. James

TEMPUS

First published 1997, reprinted 1999
Copyright © Derek N. James, 1997

Tempus Publishing Limited
The Mill, Brimscombe Port,
Stroud, Gloucestershire, GL5 2QG

ISBN 0 7524 0799 6

Typesetting and origination by
Tempus Publishing Limited
Printed in Great Britain by
Midway Clark Printing, Wiltshire

*For all who have followed in the footsteps
of Percival and Ernest Petter
while involved in Westland's aeroplane manufacturing business*

By the same author
Gloster Aircraft Company
Bristol Aeroplane Company
Hawker Aircraft
Dowty and the Flying Machine

Other titles in the Archive Photographs Aviation Series
Air Transport: The First Fifty Years
Avro Aircraft
Blackburn Aircraft
Boulton Paul Aircraft
De Havilland Aircraft
Filton and the Flying Machine
Hendon to Farnborough SBAC Displays 1932-1975
Junkers
Percivals Aircraft
Shorts Aircraft
Supermarine
Vickers

in preparation
Croydon Airport
Dornier
Fairey
Flight Refuelling
Handley Page
Messerschmidt
Napier
SAAB
Saunders-Roe

Contents

Prologue   7

1.   Genesis, the Oil Engine and War   9

2.   Peacetime Allsorts   19

3.   Another War   49

4.   Rotary Winged Revolution   71

5.   Cold War and Beyond   95

Sir Ernest Willoughby Petter signs a document while his twin-brother, Percival Waddams Petter, sits ready to add his signature. They were to play a major role in developing industry in Yeovil.

The life-jacketed pilot moves gingerly forward to the waiting launch after alighting in this Short 184 floatplane, one of the type built by Petter's Westland Aircraft Works in 1915-16.

Prologue

Scene: A high-level meeting in the office of one of His Majesty's Sea Lords at The Admiralty in London.

Time: One day in early April 1915, shortly after the Prime Minister, Mr Lloyd George, had announced in parliament that the war would *not* be over by Christmas – contrary to popular belief – and that there was a shortage of suitable armaments and equipment to win it. He had called for immediate action to remedy this.

In attendance: At least three Sea Lords, two other officials plus Messrs Ernest Willoughby Petter and Percival Waddams Petter.

Sea Lord No 1, 'Gentlemen, thank you for your telegram offering your factory in Yeovil to the government for the production of whatever is required'.

Mr P.W. Petter, 'We were shocked by the gravity of the situation'.

Sea Lord No 2, 'Our great need is for seaplanes. Are you willing to make them?'

Mr E.W. Petter, 'Our factory and experience are not exactly in line with your requirements – but we're willing to attempt anything which will help the country'.

Sea Lords, 'Good! You're the fellows we want; we'll send you the drawings and give you all the help you want. Get on with it!'

Curtain.

'So we got on with it' wrote Sir Ernest Petter, some twenty-one years later, when describing this historic meeting in the 15 September 1936 issue of *Petter's Monthly News*.

To discover how well the company has 'got on with it' ever since, please read on. But first, turn your 'thought-switch' to Victorian mode.

Yeovil's High Street and the ironmonger's shop which young James Bazeley Petter received as a wedding present from his father in 1868.

One

Genesis, the Oil Engine and War

It was in 1868 that a young Somerset man, James Bazeley Petter, received an ironmonger's business – Haman and Gillett in Yeovil – as a wedding present from his father. While James was occupied with the shop, his wife was equally busy caring for their fifteen children, among them twin boys – Percival Waddams and Ernest Willoughby – who were destined to play a major role in the future development of industry in Yeovil.

Their father expanded and diversified his business interests by building agricultural equipment. He then bought the Yeovil Foundry and Engineering Works and produced castings for the Nautilus patented fire grate, which Queen Victoria had had installed in her chilly homes at Osborne House on the Isle of Wight and at Balmoral. On leaving school Percy worked in his father's foundry. One day he read an article in *Boys' Own Paper* titled 'How to build an Oil Engine' which he showed to Ben Jacobs, the foreman who said, 'I can build a better one than that'. And he did. He also built one to power a 'horseless carriage' which was so successful that another Petter company, the Yeovil Motor Car and Cycle Co., was formed with a new factory at Reckleford. Percy remembered a distinguished colonel asking Ernest how car sales were progressing. 'Oh, we're still pushing them' replied Ernest. 'Yes, you usually are when I see you out with one' quipped the colonel.

During the latter half of the nineteenth century, Somerset saw many aeronautical events resulting from pioneering work by John Stringfellow and William Henson who lived at Chard. These excited the Petter boys who built a 'flying bicycle' – but it wouldn't. Percy built a powered rotating vertical shaft with four cruciform arms carrying box kites to experiment with vertical lift. This foreshadowed the advent of rotary-winged flight at Yeovil half a century later.

By 1910 Petter Ltd was making oil engines in many sizes and a new factory was planned at West Hendford. One afternoon in 1913, Percy Petter, his wife and two small daughters went there for a turf-cutting ceremony. As the site was west of Yeovil Mrs Petter chose the name 'Westland' for the proposed factory and garden village for its employees. With the outbreak of the 1914-18 war oil engine production soared. However, as the prologue relates, the company was also to enter the aircraft business having been told 'get on with it' by the Sea Lords.

As part of the aircraft production 'learning curve', Percy visited Shorts' Rochester factory in Kent to see what was involved in making wooden aeroplanes; 'My heart nearly failed me' he said. To smooth the transition Robert Bruce, former manager of the British and Colonial Aircraft Co. at Filton, was recruited to manage the aircraft business, starting with production of a dozen Short 184 floatplanes. Clearly, a new name was needed for this part of the Petter organisation. There is a romantic little story about this. One day Ernest Petter and two staff members walked down to the corner of a field near Yeovil where there was a small farm hut. He opened the door and solemnly announced, 'This is the Westland Aircraft Works'. Presumably he remembered the name Percy's wife had chosen for the factory and garden village.

Robert Bruce's first job was to employ draughtsmen and craftsmen. He enlisted his wife's help in preparing drawings for assembly jigs, thus making her the British aircraft industry's first female jig and tool draughtsman! In June 1915 he went to Sheerness to make drawings of the Short 184. The first aircraft was completed in December and on 1 January 1916, it left the

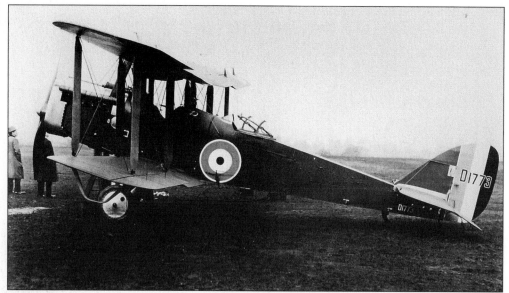

A total of 175 DH4s were ordered into sub-contract production at Yeovil but only about 150 were built. This one, D1773, was the 57th to come off the line in 1917.

factory on three horse-drawn carts and was taken to Yeovil junction for the rail journey to Hamble for flight testing. The fourth Short 184, the remains of which are in the Fleet Air Arm Museum at RNAS Yeovilton, flew in the Battle of Jutland during May-June 1916. Flown by Flt Lt F.J. Rutland ('Rutland of Jutland') and operating from a seaplane carrier in bad weather, he spotted a large fleet of enemy ships. They were followed and their position and course were reported to the British Grand Fleet – a major milestone in naval aviation history. A second sub-contract for twenty Short 166 floatplanes was completed in July, but Westland was busy buying Northover Fields to create an aerodrome. It was completed in time for flight testing of 125 Sopwith 1½ Strutter bombers and fighters built by the company. Meanwhile, Westland was building its first design, the N.1B naval fighter floatplane. Then the 'Anchor-Clankers' – the Royal Navy – changed their minds about this type of fighter so only two were built.

Early in 1917 the sub-contract floodgates opened wider for Westland. First came orders from the Aircraft Manufacturing Company (Airco) for 175 de Havilland DH4s, then 300 DH9 bombers. Because the latter type's performance with a 290 hp Siddeley Puma engine was inferior to the DH4 it was decided to fit a bigger one. Demand for the Rolls-Royce Eagle had exceeded production so the 400 hp US-built Liberty engine was substituted. Because Airco was too busy to undertake the necessary airframe redesign work, Westland got the job. The result was the DH9A, known universally as the Ninack, of which Westland built 400 of the total production of 900.

During 1917 Westland designed and built five examples of a small fighter to meet the RAF Type 1 requirement. Although named the Wagtail, its other end provided the problems where its fault-prone ABC Wasp engine was its undoing. The ABC Dragonfly engine in the 1917 Weasel two-seat fighter was another disaster. When Westland pilot Stuart Keep was flying a Weasel with Robert Bruce as passenger, the engine stopped a long way from home. Bruce leaned far out of the cockpit and cranked the starter magneto on the fuselage side – but the Dragonfly wouldn't start. Fortunately Keep managed to glide the aircraft back to the airfield. Small wonder that production stopped at only four aircraft. In September 1918 a new erecting shop was built for the sub-contract production of twenty-five big Vickers Vimy twin-engined bombers – and is still in use as part of the Normalair-Garrett facilities.

N.16, the first of two Westland N.1B floatplane fighters, was the first aircraft designed and built by the company. Note the short main floats and the one under the tail plus the two small bombs.

A one horse-power cart, loaded with Short 166 wings, on its slow way from the factory to the LSWR junction at Yeovil.

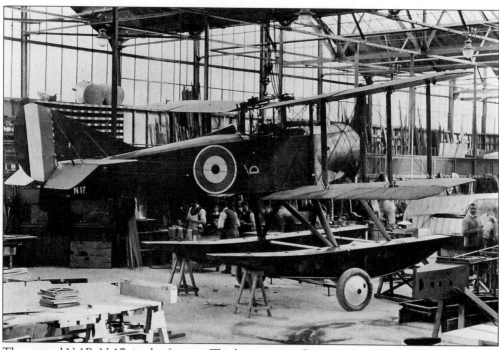

The second N.1B, N.17, in the factory. The longer main floats made the tail float unnecessary. The .303 inch machine gun on the top centre-section fired over the propeller.

It was photograph time for the members of Westland's Fitting Shop one day in 1918...

... and for the staff of the Fuselage Department.

The DH9, the DH4s bigger brother, followed it onto Westland factory production lines. This one, B7664, seen after conversion to a DH9A may have been the prototype of this variant and is pictured here at Yeovils grass airfield.

With a DH4 as a backdrop, the Tool Room staff of 1918 were photographed near to one of the canvas Bessoneaux hangars on the airfield.

Designed in 1917-18, the Wagtail light fighter for the fledgeling RAF later met the newly-formed Air Ministry's Type I Specification. Its highly unreliable ABC Wasp engine led to its undoing – like all other Wasp-powered aircraft.

The Wagtail's business end. A good view of the twin .303 inch Vickers guns, ring-and-bead sight and the 'skylight' cut in the upper wing for improved pilot visibility.

Yeovil, May 1918. This burnt-out canvas Bessoneaux hangar, a destroyed Sopwith Pup and a badly damaged Wagtail resulted from an employee's attempt to prove he could extinguish a lighted cigarette in a can of petrol.

Still in Royal Flying Corps khaki uniform and puttees, this RAF pilot climbs aboard H5080, a new Westland-built Vickers Vimy bomber, which has its Rolls-Royce Eagle engines running.

Vickers Vimys, with H5080 and '81 nearest the doors of the 140 ft span new 'Vimy hangar' at Yeovil. Note the circular windows, believed to be unique in hangar design.

The 1918 Weasel two-seat fighter was an enlarged Wagtail. Its ABC Dragonfly engine was a disaster in every way and only four Weasels were built. This second one shows the gunner's Scarff ring, upper centre-section 'skylight' and cut-away lower wing root.

While Petter's Aircraft Department was cutting its teeth on new designs young Henry Bird, a Petter apprentice (extreme left) was cutting his teeth on the manufacture of the company's traditional products – the oil engine, of which two examples are seen in this photograph taken around 1919.

Two

Peacetime Allsorts

The Armistice in November 1918 caused massive cancellation of aircraft orders – but DH9A production was allowed to continue at Yeovil where Arthur Davenport, Westland's chief draughtsman, was designing the Limousine, a small transport aircraft described by *Flight* magazine as 'combining the qualities of a luxurious motorcar and a yacht'. A report in *Country Life* read 'there was something piquant about looking at clouds in this lolling style from a cushioned armchair from behind a plate glass window... and to eat one's sandwich and smoke one's cigar while traversing ethereal kingdoms of loveliness has a voluptuous impudence which sharpens one's pleasure oddly'. No report on Concorde has been written so eloquently! Eight Limousines were built and served in Britain and Newfoundland.

The Royal Navy, plus the Armstrong Whitworth and Blackburn Aircraft companies, had all had a stab at producing a three-seat spotter-reconnaissance aircraft, using the same DH9A airframe, before Davenport created the definitive design in 1920. As a result the Walrus, of which thirty were built for the RAF, was the ugliest aeroplane produced by Westland.

Drawing heavily on the wing designs of a Russian immigrant and on earlier German cantilever monoplane wing construction, as well as using some empirical design methods (which was a mistake), Bruce and Davenport created the big Dreadnought. It crashed only seconds after its first take-off with pilot Keep losing both legs, on 9 May 1924. In the meantime, during October 1923, Juan de la Cierva y Cordoniu, the Spanish autogiro pioneer, gave Petter's board an opportunity to enter the rotary-wing field with an invitation to help finance one of his new designs. The answer was firmly 'negative'.

Unable to choose between a biplane or monoplane design to enter the Air Ministry's 1924 Light Aeroplane Competition at Lympne, Westland built both: the 439 lb biplane Woodpigeon and the Widgeon high-wing monoplane. The latter proved superior in the air and twenty-six were built. With its next aeroplane Westland got its baptism of commercial fire in a four-cornered fight with the Bristol, Hawker and Handley Page companies to win an order for a day bomber. Westland's Yeovil single-engined biplane of 1925 had few outstanding features to commend it and Hawker's Horseley got the nod.

Meanwhile, at Devil's Rest Bottom, Sussex, a tailless glider had made its first flight. Its designer, builder and pilot was Capt Geoffrey Hill who was to be the main spring behind an eight-year Westland programme of producing a family of similar aircraft – the Pterodactyls. (The name stemmed from the Greek word meaning winged finger, given to the tailless pteranodons which flapped their leathery way over Earth some 150 million years ago.) The Pterodactyl I, with a 34 hp engine, flew in November 1925. It was to lead to Westland's development of others of the same configuration.

It was at about this time that young Harald Penrose joined Westland. He was to make a major contribution to Westland's fortunes and to test flying generally.

Under Bruce's leadership there was a happy family atmosphere at Westland; so much so that, in their spare time, the Design Office staff produced a parasol monoplane design which was built as a private venture. This was the Wizard which, in 1926, had a phenomenal rate of climb; however, despite modest Air Ministry financial support, it was abandoned. At about this time the Ministry was becoming exercised over France's use of large calibre guns in its bombers. This led to a call for twin-engined fighters with two automatic 37 mm shell-firing guns to oppose them. Westland submitted the twin-engined Westbury, a real bruiser of an aircraft, with two Coventry Ordnance Works (COW) guns. Two prototypes were built (the first flying in

The first Rolls-Royce Falcon-powered four-seat Limousine, photographed between 20 April and 22 July 1919 when its interim civil registration, K-126, was carried. Note the open off-set pilot's cockpit and long exhaust pipe.

September 1926) and the guns were fired in flight – where one neatly removed the fabric from part of the top wing! But the Air Ministry's interest had wandered off in another direction and development stopped.

In 1927 the Royal Air Force needed a new general purpose 'do-it-all' aeroplane to replace the ageing DH9A; this was an era of tight government purse strings. Seven manufacturers responded to the call, Westland, with the Wapiti, being the front runner with its experience of DH9A design and production. This was recognised with an order for twenty-five Wapitis. But before production began another Westland prototype, the Witch high altitude day bomber, first flew. One of four contenders for the order, a combination of engine and handling problems ruled it out.

Westland realised that production of all-metal airframes would differ from building wooden aircraft. Thus, every stage of Wapiti design and build was geared to ensure that the change from 'wood butchering' to 'tin bashing' could be made without changing the workforce. An early factory innovation was the use of a track assembly line. Thus began an era of prosperity at Yeovil with Westland enlarging its design office and factory. During a five year period over 550 Wapitis were built for the RAF and for export to four other countries.

By 1928 Westland's experience of civil aircraft was limited, but this didn't stop Bruce and Davenport designing a small six-seater transport. This was the Westland IV which combined Davenport's philosophy of 'a monoplane is always better than a biplane' with that of other designers who believed that the ideal number of engines for a passenger aircraft was 'more than two and less than four'. Only two Westland IVs were built before a developed version, the Wessex, was produced. Ten were built in total and saw service in Britain – where they flew for Railway Air Services – in Belgium, Egypt and Rhodesia.

While these mini-airliners were in production from 1929, other Westland prototypes first got airborne. First was the Interceptor, a fast-climbing fighter to engage the enemy at 20,000 ft. It scared test pilot Louis Paget by insisting on performing a roll-off-the top of every loop! He called it, among other things, a 'flying corkscrew'; engine handling also caused problems. None of the eight contenders for this contract was ordered.

In contrast was the Pterodactyl IV, a three-seat variable-geometry cabin aircraft. Its main feature was its swing-wing. Harald Penrose's first flight nearly ended in disaster when a hump in the Yeovil airfield bumped the aircraft into the air in a stalled condition. Dutch roll developed but Harald skilfully recovered control. Its modest performance prevented it from entering production. The PV3 prototype of 1931 failed to win orders as a three-seat torpedo-bomber; however, it won fame as one of two Westland aeroplanes used by the 1933 Houston Mount Everest Expedition to make the first flight over the world's highest mountain. Designed almost simultaneously with the Interceptor was the single-seat COW gun fighter. Armed with a fearsome upwards-firing 37 mm COW piece, its development ended when the Air Ministry's ideas on aircraft armament once again changed course.

While Wapiti production was in full swing during 1930-31, Davenport designed its successor, the Wallace. This became the first RAF aircraft with an enclosed cabin for the pilot and observer/gunner. Over 170 were built for the RAF. The prototype, suitably modified, was to accompany the PV3 to India for the Mount Everest flights. In 1935 a Wallace played an important role in radar development when Robert Watson-Watt, the 'father' of radar, was tracking it on early trials at Orfordness. When the Wallace's echo faded on his screen as the aircraft flew out of range, he watched for it to reappear. Suddenly he saw a second 'blip' – which promptly split into two. He was mystified until the Wallace landed and the pilot reported that he had seen a formation of three Hawker Harts which had divided into two. This was Watson-Watts' first confirmation of being able to use radar to assess the size of formations of aircraft.

The next four designs, built only as prototypes, differed widely in concept. The high wing of the PV7 General Purpose monoplane suffered from torsional weakness and twisted in flight. When Davenport appeared sceptical Harald Penrose put him in the rear cockpit and demonstrated the twist in the air. 'Stop Harald!' he cried, 'You'll have the ruddy wings off!' When a wing did break off in a dive, Harald miraculously escaped through a small cockpit window and parachuted to safety with only some bruising and the embarrassing loss of all his trouser buttons. This was the first parachute escape from the enclosed cockpit of a British aircraft. Next into the air was the F.7/30 biplane fighter. It featured an engine buried in the fuselage behind the pilot and turning the propeller through a long drive shaft. Apart from occasionally catching fire after being rolled, its officially-specified evaporatively-cooled Rolls-Royce Goshawk engine was its undoing. The Pterodactyl V, the last of the family, was a two-seat turret fighter which demanded all of Penrose's skill during its year-long flight test programme. As a research aircraft it provided a wealth of knowledge about flight in tailless aircraft but it did not provide Westland with a production order, and development was abandoned in February 1936.

The C.29 autogyro was Westland's first rotary-winged aircraft. It was a disaster, exhibiting heavy ground resonance with the rotor turning and rotor vibrations when taxiing. When Juan de la Cierva came to Yeovil to test fly it he said that 'it would be unwise to try'. No solutions to the problems could be found and this project also was abandoned.

A board room battle resulted in the resignations of Robert Bruce and Geoffrey Hill and pushed Edward 'Teddy' Petter, the son of Sir Ernest Petter, up the promotion ladder to technical director. In spite of Bruce's departure and the C.29's failure, Westland's interest in rotating wings was undiminished. Both Penrose and young Petter were interested in them and regarded them as a challenge. Davenport too, saw their future applications. Thus, with his backing, 'Teddy' Petter designed the CL.20 autogyro which first flew in February 1935. Having completed eighty test flights it was abandoned six months later with insuperable lift and control problems. In that year Westland Aircraft Works ceased to be a branch of Petters Ltd and operated as a separate company named Westland Aircraft Ltd. In this new guise the company moved up a gear.

As its name implied, luxury was all-important in the Limousine I's cabin which was button-back lined, carpeted and had thick upholstered seats The pilot's cockpit is on the left.

Limousine on ice. Sydney Cotton's big six-seater Limousine III, G-EARV, being prepared for a seal-spotting sortie from Botwood, Newfoundland in 1921. Its size is emphasised by the people around it.

Clearly the offspring – somewhere along the line – of the DH.9A, the Walrus was an untidy aeroplane. The forward hydrovane, arrester-wire grippers and the ventral observation pannier are noteworthy unsightly additions.

'A vicious beast' was test pilot Stuart Keep's March 1921 description of the Walrus. With flotation bags inflated, the first one reveals some of its drag-producing airframe's excrescences – plus the Napier Lion engine's external 'plumbing'.

The inclined windows and door show how the very thick wing of the 1924 Dreadnought was blended into the fuselage. Note the sharp fore-and-aft 'chine' where the sloping rear fuselage sides join the underside. Insufficient knowledge of aerodynamics was this 70 ft span aeroplane's undoing.

The only known photograph of the Dreadnought airborne. It was taken only seconds before it crashed after take-off on its first flight at Yeovil on 9 May 1924.

Wreckage of Dreadnought's front end after the crash. The engine, with exhaust pipe still attached, was driven back through the cockpit almost to the wing leading edge. Pilot Stuart Keep lost both legs – but survived.

Weighing only 439 lb (graphically demonstrated here) the Woodpigeon was built for the 1924 Air Ministry light aeroplane trials at Lympne. Placed second in the Grosvenor Challenge race, its detail design and use of Bristol's 32 hp Cherub engine were criticised.

The parasol monoplane Widgeon, also built for the light aeroplane trials, proved superior to the biplane Woodpigeon. Built in 1928, Widgeon III, VH-UHU (with a spurious registration for a film) is seen flying in Australia in 1990. Good on ya, sport!

Three Yeovil day bombers were built; this last one flew in June 1926. Although they failed to win orders all three earned their corn as research aircraft. Note the over-wing fuel tanks on J7510.

Well, this wing shape is still around today, but the Pterodactyl 1's wing-tip elevons – named 'controllers' in 1926 – and its 34 hp Bristol Cherub pusher engine are rarely seen on modern RAF aircraft!

A 'spare-time' design by Westland, the one-off 1926 Wizard 'racer' needed further refinement and modification before this rather tired looking airframe/engine combination became...

... this sleek fighter project. Developed with modest Air Ministry financial support, it flew in the RAF Display at Hendon in June 1928 but its performance was not good enough to attract an order and it was abandoned.

With both 450 hp Bristol Jupiter engines running, the pilot of the first Westbury signals to the ground crew – but everyone's attention is focussed elsewhere! Note the short corrugated engine nacelle and front gunner's position.

Not everyone's idea of a fighter. This 1926 photograph of a Westbury shows its deep fuselage, lengthened engine nacelle and the ballast weights simulating the big guns.

The first of 558 production Wapiti General Purpose aircraft, J9078 is pictured in 1927. Of interest are the wing slats, neatly cowled 420 hp Bristol Jupiter engine, fuselage-side gun mounting and wind-driven generator.

'Many hundreds of thousands of brake horsepower of Petter Oil Engines are running in all parts of the world for industrial, electrical and marine purposes' reads this 1929 advertisement. Illustrated is the motor yacht *Suna* and an electricity generating plant.

'What – snow in Australia?' The skis on this Wapiti IA, the second of twenty-eight delivered to the Royal Australian Air Force during 1929, were temporarily attached for a photographer's benefit while there was snow on Yeovil's airfield.

The motto of No. 55 Squadron is 'Nothing makes us afraid' – not even flying a close-knit vic in Wapiti IIAs of the squadron's C Flight. These aircraft, up from Hinaidi, Iraq, were photographed during the early 1930s.

'Muy bien, Senor Penrose!' Harald demonstrates a float-equipped Wapiti V to an enthralled group of boater- and trilby-hatted onlookers at Argentina's San Fernando naval base. This was part of the 1931 British Exhibition in Buenos Aires.

The Witch of the Westland. The complex bow-legged outrigged undercarriage was necessary because of the Witch's fuselage bomb bay. This photograph, taken in January 1928, shows the parasol wing configuration of this high altitude bomber.

With a 70 hp Armstrong Siddeley Genet engine and spatted outrigged stabiliser wheels the Pterodactyl 1B, J9251, here carries RAF markings and is seen at Farnborough in 1928.

A unique photograph of the Interceptor, with an uncowled Bristol Mercury engine, flying at Yeovil. On the ground are Armstrong Whitworth Siskin IIIAs of No. 25 Squadron encamped on the airfield in 1930.

Yeovil, 17 July 1931. A close-up of the Interceptor's engine and robust strutted and braced undercarriage. Some pilots believed the wing bracing would collapse if the undercarriage was damaged. Note slats in wing leading edge.

Powered by three 95 hp Aircraft Disposal Company Cirrus III engines, the first Westland IV six-passenger mini-airliner stands ready for flight on 21 February 1929.

One of four Wessex sold to Belgium's Sabena airline, OO-AGE was photographed on a test flight over Somerset in 1931.

A Sabena pilot collects a Wessex from Yeovil on 2 September 1930. From left to right: Westland pilot Louis Paget, Messrs Byrom, Brunton (Westland pilot) O'Neill (Sabena UK agent), Capt Cocquyt (Sabena chief pilot) Percival Petter, Capt Stuart Keep (Westland factory superintendent).

'They don't like the cold steel up 'em Mr Mainwaring'. Nor the hot lead! The Air Ministry was more than a decade ahead of Private Jones when it called for a fighter with a big upwards-firing 37 mm gun. Westland's COW Gun Fighter first flew in December 1930.

Close-up view of the big gun installation in the COW Gun Fighter. Note the fuel tanks ahead of the cockpit and the side-mounted oil cooler.

Although a three-seat passenger aircraft, the Pterodactyl IV's wing gave it a menacing appearance. Its 'bicycle' main landing gear with outriggers and its swing wing – albeit only 4 degrees – were advanced design features when completed in March 1931.

The Pterodactyl IV's central pod contained the cabin, bicycle main undercarriage, power unit and the hand-operated swing-wing mechanism. The opening in the top surface enabled the wing root to move inboard when fully swung aft.

For the 1931 RAF Display at Hendon the Pterodactyl IV was painted to represent a fierce prehistoric monster, complete with teeth and claws, which probably had pterodactyls for breakfast 150 million years ago!

The private venture PV.3 torpedo bomber was clearly a Wapiti descendant but its neat 575 hp Bristol Pegasus engine installation and spatted wheels owe little to its ancestor. Note the window in the bomb aimer's prone position under the pilot's cockpit.

Top flight. Harald Penrose in the PV.3 after its conversion for use by the 1933 Houston Mount Everest Flying Expedition team. The photographer's enclosed cabin had hinged window panels and a glass panel in the floor.

PV.3 G-ACAZ airborne at Yeovil in January 1933. The pilot's open cockpit had a floor and was sealed internally against draughts. The cameras and film boxes were electrically-heated, as was every item of the crew's clothing and oxygen masks.

The triumvirate which helped put Westland on top of the world. In front of the Houston-Westland PV.3 after it had clambered up to over 35,000 ft in January 1933, are, from left to right: Arthur Davenport, chief designer, Harald Penrose and Robert Bruce, managing director.

With the peak of Everest in his sights, The Marquis of Douglas and Clydesdale, pilot of the Houston-Westland PV.3, with Col Stewart Blacker his observer/photographer, prepares to make history with the first flight over the mountain top on 3 April 1933. This amazing photograph was taken by Mr Bonnett of the Gaumont-British Film Corporation, in the accompanying Westland Wallace flown by Flt Lt David McIntyre.

Peak performance. Once Wapiti G-AAWA, then the PV.6/Wallace prototype, this aeroplane was modified to the same standard as the PV.3 for use by the 1933 Everest Expedition. Here, photographed from the PV.3, it flies high over the Himalayas.

The first production Wallace I flies low at Yeovil in November 1932. Note the 550 hp Bristol Pegasus, spatted wheels, wing slats and two open cockpits. The first 80 Wallace Is and IIs were all converted Wapitis.

With enclosed cockpits, this aircraft led the first big production batch of 75 Wallace IIs in 1935. They were all newly built, from propeller spinner to rear light.

Originally built with an open pilot's cockpit, the PV7 General Purpose aircraft carries a 1,000 lb torpedo, required when operating as a coastal reconnaissance and torpedo-bomber. It first flew on 30 October 1933.

The company's first rotary-winged aeroplane, the five-seat C.29 autogyro is seen in 1934. Sadly, ground resonance problems were too complex to be solved. The C.29 was broken up at RAE Farnborough in June 1939.

Seven manufacturers fought for orders for fighters built to the F.7/30 Specification. Westland's unusual biplane with its gull upper wing, enclosed cockpit and disastrous evaporatively-cooled Goshawk engine buried in the fuselage was not the winner.

The F7/30's 600 hp Goshawk installation showing the long drive-shaft, reduction gear, original exhausts, forward cockpit and upper wing attachments in one of Rolls-Royce's test beds in Derby.

In its initial unclothed state the Pterodactyl V turret-fighter reveals its wing and fuselage structure, 600 hp Goshawk engine, main landing gear and trailing balancer skids.

The Pterodactyl V in RAF markings has larger wing-tip rudders and underwing fins. The robust lower wing had struts and other bits of kit attached to it. No photographs of this aircraft with the turret fitted have been discovered

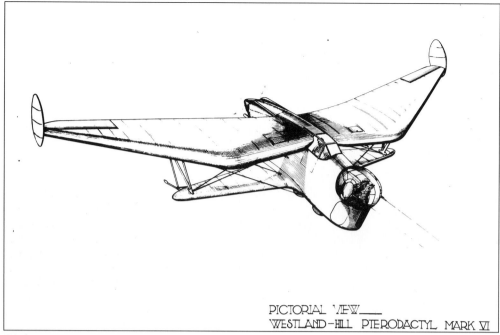

PICTORIAL VIEW___
WESTLAND−HILL PTERODACTYL MARK VI

With a nose gun turret the Pterodactyl VI two-seat fighter project of 1933, of necessity, had its Rolls-Royce Kestrel engine installed as a pusher unit. Designed to an Air Ministry F.5/33 Specification it never got off the drawing board.

The CL20 autogyro, seen in early 1935, was Westland's second attempt to enter the rotary winged field. It, too, failed to make the grade. Standing on the left is Oliver Reed, Flight Shed Foreman.

Three

Another War

With the support of the powerful Roy Fedden at the Bristol Aeroplane Co., who was promoting the use of his radial engines, Westland submitted an eight-gun fighter design to Specification F5/34; but Petter still had to prove himself to the Air Ministry and contracts went to the Gloster Aircraft and Bristol Aeroplane companies. However, in 1935, Westland's submission to meet the need for an Army Cooperation aircraft won an order for two prototypes using the proven parasol wing configuration. It also resulted in a series of orders over the next seven years into the Second World War era, during which 1,652 Lysanders – as this aircraft was named – were built. This was to be Westland's largest ever production order. The Lysander was used in a variety of roles and experimental configurations but has become best known for its clandestine spy-dropping-and-collecting operations deep into Occupied Europe. It was licence-built in Canada and was flown by the RAF and six other air forces, including the US Army Air Force.

Petter's next design to enter production was the Whirlwind twin-engined single-seat fighter to meet Specification F37/35. Armed with four 20 m cannon in the nose it was full of novel design features. 'Too full for its own good' one test pilot remarked. These included routing the exhaust pipes through the fuel tanks, interconnecting the wing flaps with the leading-edge radiator shutters, a high set tailplane, hydraulic throttle controls and the use of the Rolls-Royce Peregrine in-line engine. Large production orders were placed but were gradually cut back as development flying dragged on and on. The Whirlwind's manoeuvrability and high-speed handling were questionable, the controls were not well harmonised and the engines overheated on the ground. It was a poor bet as a fighter and was moved to the fighter-bomber role. Finally, Rolls-Royce announced an end to Peregrine production so that it could concentrate on the Merlin. Thus only 116 Whirlwinds were built – some 'Whirlibombers' being used effectively by two RAF squadrons.

In January 1941 the twin-engined Welkin high altitude fighter, intended to combat expected high altitude Luftwaffe attacks on the British Isles, was accepted for production. It first flew on 1 November 1942 with Harald Penrose as pilot. Soon its very high-aspect ratio wing, 1,700 hp supercharged Merlin engines and pressurised cabin were giving him a view of Britain from around 45,000 ft, an altitude not previously reached. Sadly, the Welkin was plagued with handling problems, particularly when in a dive from altitude or when manoeuvring. By 1944, when the Luftwaffe failed to put in appearance in strength at very high altitude, the writing was on the wall. The Welkin would never enter operational service. Nevertheless, seventy-seven were built, most being scrapped at Maintenance Units.

During the war, in addition to Lysander, Whirlwind and Welkin production, Westland factories built nearly 700 Spitfires and over 1,670 Seafires and modified US-built Curtiss Mohawks, Tomahawks and Kittyhawks. Other production included eighteen Barracudas and many centre-sections for Albemarles. December 1946 saw the first flight at Boscombe Down of the Rolls-Royce Eagle piston-engined prototype Wyvern single-seat naval strike aircraft. This launched a 7 year development programme, fraught with engine and propeller control problems, before Wyverns entered service in May 1953. This was not surprising as the Eagle, the Rolls-Royce Clyde and Armstrong Siddeley Python turbo-prop engines (this last one powering the production aircraft) were new and untried. Wyverns saw operational service in the 1956 Suez Campaign. A total of 127 were built of which 40 were lost or became instructional airframes. The Wyvern was Westland's last fixed-wing aircraft. Its epitaph could be Harald Penrose's comment to the author, 'The Wyvern was very nearly a very good aircraft'.

The unfinished first prototype Lysander, in red oxide finish, minus undercarriage leg fairings, engine cowling gills and with a two-blade wooden propeller and fixed tailplane. The pointed shape on the fuselage shows the edges of four access panels in the fabric covering.

For recognition purposes the Royal Observer Corps divided aeroplanes into two groups; the Lysander and all the rest! With Harald Penrose in the cockpit, the completed prototype Lysander displays its flaps, slats, struts and spats and unusual wing which made it a unique shape in the sky.

At times the short-landing and take-off Lysander appeared an elegant flying machine with all the attributes to make it a splendid Army Cooperation aircraft. With Harald Penrose at the controls, this was one of those times.

Though reigning for only ten months before abdicating in December 1936, King Edward VIII visited several RAF Stations. Here, in June, he climbs wooden steps to inspect the prototype Lysander's cockpit at Martlesham Heath. On right of the front group, with hands behind his back, is HRH the Duke of York, soon to become King George VI.

Dubbed 'The Pregnant Perch', this Lysander had an experimental under-belly gun position for beach-strafing in case of an invasion. In June 1940, after in-flight engine failure with test pilot George Snarey aboard, it ended up with its nose in a ditch.

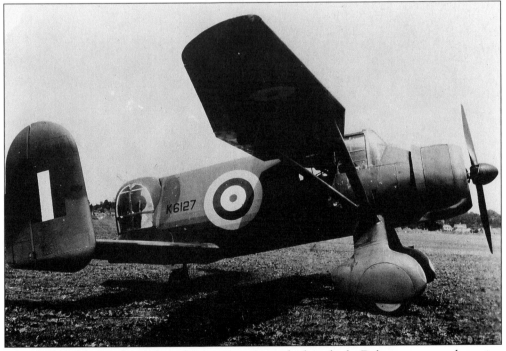

Also intended for beach-strafing, the prototype Lysander later had a Delanne-type tandem wing and mock-up four-gun tail turret. Despite its ungainly appearance Harald Penrose looped it during its first flight on 27 July 1941! Here it has a Perseus engine.

The pilot of this 'al fresco' – ie. all canopies open – No. 225 Squadron Lysander II pictured in 1940, eyeballs the camera for a splendid air-to-air shot. Wheel cover removal prevented mud clogging on grass airfields. By the time this aeroplane was built the unit price was down to £3,063 8s 5d (£3,063.42p)!

A 'cloak-and-dagger' Lysander IIIA of No. 161 Special Duty Squadron. With black undersurfaces, a long range fuel tank and side ladder, they flew clandestine agent-dropping and collecting night ops deep into Occupied Europe.

'See amid the winter's snow'. With peacetime silver finish or wartime camouflage twelve Lysander IIs, built by National Steel Car Corp. Ltd at Malton, Ontario, await delivery to the Royal Canadian Air Force in late 1939.

'Eminence Grise'. Painted dark grey, the first of only two prototype Whirlwinds built is seen in September 1938. The through-wing (and through-fuel tank) exhaust pipes above the engine nacelle and the high tailplane are noteworthy features.

The pitch of the de Havilland propeller blades shows that the first Whirlwind's 885 hp Rolls-Royce Peregrines rotate in opposite directions. The centre-section radiators, slim fuselage and 1939-40 black/white wing undersurfaces are seen to advantage.

Photographed on 7 June 1941 in front of a Whirlwind I are Group Captain HRH the Duke of Kent with Eric Mensforth, Westland's managing director. The duke was later to lose his life in the crash of a Sunderland flying boat.

Harald Penrose breaks sharply starboard during a photo-sortie. The four 20 mm cannon in the nose and the slender fuselage and engine nacelles typify the Whirlwind.

The 1941 'office': the Whirlwind I's fully-furnished cockpit, complete with Barr & Stroud gyro gunsight, hydraulic throttle controls left, control column and blind flying panel centre – minus the IFF recognition device switch in the right hand panel.

Fourteen ladies and a gentleman pictured during 1941-42. He is Robert Finch BEM, foreman at Westland's Weymouth factory in Tilley's Garage. But who are the ladies? Unfortunately there were no names on the photograph.

Wolf in sheep's clothing. Westland's 'hack' sea grey civil-registered Whirlwind. Paint tone changed aft of the cockpit due to the use of two competing companies' paint. The rear fuselage paint supplier got the order!

During 1942 the Minister of Aircraft Production, Stafford Cripps, with spectacles and holding pipe, visited Westland to be shown Spitfire production lines by Eric Mensforth, nearest the camera, the company's managing director. Ex-Petter apprentice Henry Bird watches from the aisle in the background. (See page 18)

Wet day at Westland. In its primer paint the prototype Welkin high altitude fighter is prepared for first engine runs in October 1942. Its 70 ft span wing provided temporary shelter to attendant staff.

The first Welkin's fin and rudder have been cropped and its 1,560 hp Rolls-Royce Merlin' nacelles lengthened. Here it carries two unpainted 200 gallon underwing jettisonable fuel tanks. Built to combat Luftwaffe high-flyers which didn't materialise, Welkins never entered RAF service.

Welkin in the Welkin. Pictured during April 1943, DX318, the 29th Welkin I to be built is seen with Medium Sea Grey top surfaces and P.R. Blue under surfaces. (Welkin is the poetic name for the upper air.)

Model of 'Teddy' Petter's 1943 jet fighter-bomber project. That year he left Westland to become English Electric's chief engineer, taking this and other designs with him, one of which became the Canberra.

The mighty Eagle engine, a variant of which powered the first six Wyvern prototypes, was 9 ft long. The caption to this Rolls-Royce photograph credits the Eagle with a nominal output of 3,500 hp.

This maze of timber, angle iron, plumbing and the wings off one of the last three prototypes was a Wyvern fuel system test rig for pressure fuelling and defuelling for the Wyvern Mk. 2. The rig in the foreground provided hydraulic power for the wing fold jacks.

On 15 October 1947 Westland pilot Peter Garner tragically lost his life after a propeller bearing failed in flight. The enormous drag from the eight stationary blades caused TS371, the first prototype Wyvern, to crash.

When Wyvern TF2 second prototype's Python engine appeared to flame out in flight its pilot, Mike Graves, attempted a normal landing at Yeovil. Sadly, the aircraft overshot and crashed into some houses with Graves and the inhabitants losing their lives.

During August 1953 Harald Penrose made his last flight as Westland's chief test pilot in this first production Wyvern TF2, VW872, fitted with a dihedral tailplane. Harald believed that this photograph was taken on that last flight.

A Wyvern S.4 of 703 Squadron being launched from HMS *Ark Royal*'s port steam catapult in 1955.

Gotcha! With flaps lowered a Wyvern S.4 reaches for – and is about to engage – the carrier's first arrester wire with its hook. Note the deck landing control officer's 'bats' in action.

Wyvern S.4, VZ782, of 813 Squadron, with wings folded in HMS *Eagle* during 1955. In that year folding wingtips on the Wyvern were abandoned as unnecessary.

This Wyvern S4, VZ752, has its wings folded (note the jury strut supporting the starboard wing) and a smiling R.H. Gundry in its cockpit. That was before...

... this happened. Drivers of cars think 'There's nothing in the *Highway Code* about aeroplanes'. R.H. Gundry, operating the Wyvern's brakes, thinks 'There's nothing in the *Pilot's Notes* about cars'. Cars and aeroplane met at the junction of Ilchester Road and Coombe Street Lane on 29 November 1956 while the Wyvern was being towed from Yeovil to Merryfield aerodrome.

Photographed at Westland Families' Day at Yeovil in 1975 are the sole surviving Wyvern and men who had worked on the ten pre-production Mk1 aircraft. This is VR137. They are, from left to right: Ron Jelley, Tony Holroyd, Eric Bond, Fred Ballam (who has provided much information for this book), Eric Harrington, Don Trebley, John Stone, Malgwyn Edwards, Roy Gray, Philip Tweed, John Loman and Donald Hill.

In 1956-57 Westland's Ilchester site refurbished some ex-RAF F-86 Sabre fighters. With a surplus F-86 front fuselage as a test stand, Charlie Harris in the cockpit and Bernie Rogers prepare for engine runs with the General Electric J-47 GE-13.

VZ789, a Wyvern S.4 of 827 Squadron, 'bolting' with 420 ft of HMS *Eagle*'s flight deck remaining for another take-off and go-around. It is believed that this photograph was taken during approval trials of the S.4 Wyvern.

Four

Rotary Winged
Revolution

At the very moment that the Wyvern first flew, Westland's Board was securing the high ground on which to build the company's future. This was through the bold decision to move into the new field of rotary winged aircraft. It was not taken lightly and followed deep research into every aspect of rotary wing design, production, development and operation. The second major decision was how to implement the first one. Westland chose the quicker path of licence-building an established design rather than the longer one of starting from scratch.

The path which led Westland to Sikorsky in the United States was too tortuous to describe in these pages, as were the negotiations and discussions between the two companies. Suffice it to say that, in January 1947, Sikorsky granted Westland a licence to build the S-51 helicopter. This set in train a great transfer of drawings to Westland from Sikorsky and their anglicisation before they could be issued to the shop floor. The magnitude of this task was greatly underrated. Oliver Fitzwilliams, who joined the company in March 1947 as helicopter engineer and was made responsible for all design and development work on them, has recorded that when Alan Bristow flew the first Westland-built WS-51 on 5 December 1948, there were only fourteen people, including the secretary and the office boy, in the department. Subsequently, 139 of these helicopters were built for civil use and for the RN and RAF, where they were named Dragonfly. For nine weeks during 1950-51 British European Airways used them for the world's first scheduled and sustained helicopter passenger service linking Cardiff, Wrexham and Liverpool. A Westland development of the WS-51 was the Widgeon, of which only a handful were built

While the helicopter was at Yeovil to stay, Westland's project office devised swept-winged jet-powered Wyverns, a four-jet airliner and a side-by-side basic jet trainer. But Fitzwilliams' desire to build a larger and more advanced helicopter would not be denied and this led to production of the Sikorsky WS-55, renamed Whirlwind.

This near-400 aircraft programme established Westland as a front rank helicopter company. Whirlwinds were produced in twelve different variants for civil and military use. They flew as communications and anti-submarine aircraft, as passenger and cargo transports, equipped the Royal Flight and were exported to half-a-dozen countries.

The success of later Whirlwind variants with turboshaft engines inspired Westland to prepare plans to instal them in Sikorsky S-58s to meet Royal Navy needs for a large anti-submarine warfare (ASW) helicopter. Thus the Wessex was created, of which more than 300 were produced in ten variants for military and civil operations.

In November 1954 Eric Mensforth, Westland's managing director, had revealed the company's intention to build a large helicopter as a private venture and to name it Westminster. Clearly his words were aimed at the place where he hoped to enlist support for this 87 ft long, 15 ton monster. When doubts were raised about its size, Fitzwilliams dismissed them with the comment that it was 'simply a small helicopter drawn on larger sheets of paper'! Unfortunately Westland came under pressure from the Royal Navy's top brass to abandon the Westminster. They believed that work on this big aeroplane would slow development of their much needed ASW Wessex. There was, too, a threat from the Fairey Rotodyne – a noisy beast,

First of the Many. Westland's first helicopter, G-AKTW, the anglicised Sikorsky S-51. It led the way towards the company's production of some 2,300 helicopters to date.

God wot, with its tip-jet propulsion system – which was in the same category and was a more advanced design. For these reasons only two prototype Westminsters had been built when work was halted in 1961. However, Fitzwilliams was already producing proposals and drawings for 400-seater helicopters. There was no lack of self-confidence at Yeovil!

Following the government's 1957 Defence White Paper, which had ruled out development of fighter aircraft beyond the English Electric P.1 Lightning and pointed the way towards rationalisation of the aircraft industry, it was made clear that the government wanted one helicopter manufacturing organisation centred on Yeovil. It was in August 1959 that Westland began the piecemeal acquisition of Britain's other helicopter manufacturers. First came Saunders-Roe, bringing with it its Scout and Wasp, Black Knight space rocket and hovercraft programmes; then Bristol and the Belvedere, both companies amicably joining forces with Westland. Finally came Fairey – kicking and screaming – with its Rotodyne and the AEW Gannet. Apart from the facilities, personnel and hardware, Westland also gained the services of a number of outstanding technical, commercial and management personalities from these companies. Subsequently, 149 Scouts and 98 Wasps were built for the Army, RN and nine other countries' air arms.

But before the 2,300 finished articles, the components had first to be built. The original photograph's caption reveals that bits for this first all-British Dragonfly rotor head were made at Turner Bros. in Wolverhampton. Now – is this Wolverhampton or Yeovil? On the extreme right is Arthur Angerson; third from the right is Arthur Wyatt.

This Dragonfly 1, VZ962, served with 705 Squadron for trials of the winch which is seen attached to the port side of the pylon. This aircraft can be seen in the International Helicopter Museum at Weston-super-Mare.

In 1947 British European Airways' Helicopter Unit was based at Yeovil for seven months experimental flying with S-51s G-AJOV, 'OR and G-AKCU and Bell 47B-3s G-AKFA and 'B seen with the Unit's staff.

Westland's Transmission Shop during the early 1950s with Dragonfly and Whirlwind gear box and rotor head assembly work in progress. From the left to right are Frank ?, Bill Hutchings, Ted White, Keith Griffiths, George Kircup, Bob Wilds, Tom Staddon, Stan Scanes and George McCullough.

Not an experiment in solid fuel for helicopters! The small smoking chimney apparently protruding from the back of this WS-51, readied for delivery to Italy in April 1951, belongs to a company incinerator used to destroy confidential waste.

Registered LN-ORG, this WS-51 Mk 1A was sold to Norway in October 1952, but it came back home again to Westland as G-AMRE before being written off in March 1957.

With the scent of victory in their nostrils, the Production Control Department team, finalists in the 1953 Interdepartmental Skittles Competition, pose for a photograph. From left to right are Les Waine, Jack Baker, Vic Dash, Ron Job, Joe Choat, Bob Hamilton, –?-.

On 17 June 1954 the first official helicopter landing was made at London's South Bank. The *Evening News* chartered a WS-51 from Westland to take aerial views of London for the paper, copies of which were flown back to Yeovil by John Fay, Westland's test pilot, here seen receiving them.

The Widgeon gave Westland some hands-on experience of helicopter design. Executair's Widgeon, photographed at Yeovil in July 1959, later became Westland's 'hack'. It was withdrawn from use in September 1975.

Westland used XA866, fifth production Whirlwind 1 for undercarriage development work. It has a straight tailcone and anhedral tailplane.

HRH Prince Philip visits Westland. He is seen here with managing director Edward Wheeldon, meeting some of the company's senior executives. From left to right: Harald Penrose (group sales manager and special director), Ted Boulger (group contracts manager and special director), Tony Hobbs, Ted Frost, -?-, Mac Swinburne (group works engineer).

Production of Whirlwinds established Westland as a first rate helicopter company. This Whirlwind 10 winches up a 'survivor' during an RAF practice air-sea rescue mission. Note its drooped tailcone and flat tailplane.

The 'Anchor Clankers' – aka the Royal Navy – are major operators of Westland helicopters. This Whirlwind 7, XL853, belonging to RNAS Yeovilton's Station Flight, was seen there in 1967.

Civil Whirlwinds were designated WS-55s. This British European Airways Series 1 aircraft flew service trials on the Waterloo Heliport-London Heathrow route along the Thames – hence the floats in case of an emergency alighting.

Shell Refining Company's WS-55 Series 1 was fitted with inflatable pontoons which were lighter and more easily repairable than metal floats. It is seen here in Bahrein during 1956.

One of only two Whirlwind 8s built, in 1959, for the Queen's Flight, XN127 is pictured at Woolsington-Newcastle Airport. They had dual controls and the four-seat cabin was specially furnished and soundproofed.

A trio of Gnome turbo-shaft-powered Whirlwind 10s built for the Royal Air Force's search-and-rescue squadrons, hover in line-abreast formation at Yeovil before delivery.

Westland in an east land. RAF Whirlwind 10 of Far East Air Force lands at a remote Borneo village in 1964. Although the place appears deserted, nine people can be discerned in this photograph – with a magnifying glass!

Although described as 'just a small helicopter drawn on bigger pieces of paper' the 87 ft long Westminster was Westland's largest helicopter with a 72 ft diameter main rotor and weighing 36,000 lb loaded. The prototype is here tied down for engine running during June 1958.

In reality a flying test rig, the Westminster was a steel-tube space frame with the cockpit, engines, rotors and transmission systems positioned as for a passenger helicopter not then designed. The central 'black box' is the flight test auto-observer cover.

G-APLE, the first Westminster, wearing its terylene 'skin' which certainly gave it more visual appeal. Noteworthy features are the external fuel tanks and the six-bladed rotor.

The second Westminster, here seen airborne in 1959, had a redesigned structure and nose. The whole programme was abandoned when the Royal Navy complained that Westminster work was delaying Wessex development. The Wessex flew five months ahead of schedule.

Westland's spin test rig for helicopter pulse jets tucked away in a Somerset quarry to minimise environmental pollution by noise.

Scene at Weston-super-Mare's Old Mixon factory, previously owned by Bristol Helicopters Ltd, in 1963. A brace of Bristols (Belvedere and Sycamore – the latter bearing the Westland name) and three Westland Whirlwind 10s are evident.

Cricket at Old Mixon; the Shop 6 Under 40s v Over 40s. From left to right, front row: Bob Trump, Colin Weekes, Bob Trenner, Jack Badman, -?-, -?-, Billy Wright, Harry Haskett, -?-, Bill Burrows, Wilf Pearce. Back row: 'Chalky' White, Colin Weekes' son, Arthur Evans, Bill Thurslake, Fred Stapleton, Trevor -?-, John Winchester, Mike Taylor, Colin Wilkins, Eric Densley, -?-.

Beginning in 1964, after the Bell Model 47 was chosen for British Army use and named Sioux AH.1, Westland built 250 at the Yeovil factory with the lengthy designation WA-B47G-3B-4. This one was the second off the line.

Wessex 2s carrying underslung loads while acting in the close support role to ground troops.

The Wessex can carry up to sixteen fully-equipped troops. Here it is picking up a border patrol in Northern Ireland in April 1965.

XT256, seen in 1966, was the second of three development Wessex 3s used for trials before release for Service use. The 'horsecollar' fairing smoothed air flow round the radome which had affected the tail rotor causing airframe 'twitch'.

The Great G-ATBY? Receiving its first Wessex 60 Series 1s in September 1966, Bristow Helicopters Ltd ultimately operated a fleet of nineteen of them. Note the pop-out flotation gear on the main undercarriage wheels.

A Bristow Helicopters' Wessex 60 enables work to be carried out on the Royal Sovereign light tower in the English Channel. Bristow was contracted to Trinity House for lighthouse support operations.

An Army Air Corps Scout 1, XT614, built by Westland's Fairey Aviation Division at Hayes. It is pictured on patrol in Malaysia with Wasp-style flotation gear.

Armed with four Vigilant anti-tank missiles, Scout 1, XT642, hovers in the ground cushion.

Nimbus al fresco. Access to the Scout and Wasp's Bristol Siddeley Nimbus turboshaft engine was 100 per cent. This Scout, minus main rotor, arrived on a special handling trolley at the 1962 SBAC Farnborough Show.

XP189, the fifth of a development batch of eight Scout 1s, was used for a range of flight trials including those of this Lynx semi-rigid main rotor during 1970-74.

Through an Anglo-French agreement, Westland's Yeovil and Old Mixton factories built 262 Sud SA 341 Gazelle trainer/utility aircraft, the first flying in April 1970. *The Sharks*, the RN's aerobatic display team from RNAS Culdrose, fly Gazelles.

A Gazelle 1 of 4 Regiment Army Air Corps pictured in 1987. Note the fenestron – a form of enclosed variable pitch fan – which replaces the conventional tail rotor.

The second type of French helicopter built by Westland was the SA330 Puma transport, the first of which got airborne on November 1970. This 1982 photograph shows Puma top structures in production in Shop 7 at Old Mixon where four were built.

Last of the four dozen Westland-built Pumas built for the RAF.

Big stinger. Wasp 1, XT431, carries two under-fuselage Mk 44 torpedoes. Note the splayed wheels to provide greater stability and to combat ship motion when on the deck.

This Wasp, about to land on a frigate's aft platform, has a missile launching rail mounted well outboard on its starboard side. The ship's wake appears to indicate that it had just manoeuvred to face into wind.

A Royal Navy rating gets to grips with some minor servicing on this Wasp's Nimbus engine. The palm tree in the background suggests that it is ashore at some sub-tropical base. It could be Torquay, of course!

XV370, the first Sikorsky-built SH3D Sea King delivered in October 1966 to Westland as a 'pattern' aircraft. The large inflatable 'trousers' in the foreground are its flexible fuel tank.

Black ties were *de rigeur* for this gathering of test pilots for John Fay's retirement in 1968. From left to right: Peter Wilson, Slim Sear, John Fay, Harry Smith (A.T.C.O.), Leo de Vigne, Ron Gellatly, Keith Chadbourne, Ron Crayton and Mike Ginn.

Five
Cold War and Beyond

In the early 1960s the Royal Navy was seeking a large long-range submarine hunter-killer helicopter. Soviet Russia had earlier embarked on a major programme of building large numbers of nuclear and conventionally-powered submarines, and these were already operating in the world's oceans where they were being encountered with increasing frequency. This led to the production of a heavily anglicised version of the Sikorsky S-61 Sea King powered with two (Bristol Siddeley) Rolls-Royce Gnome turboshaft engines. This aeroplane entered service in August 1969. It has since been operated by a dozen or more air arms. Production ceased with the 330th being handed over to the Royal Norwegian Air Force on 10 May 1996 for service with 330 Squadron, RNoAF. All Sea King work was then moved to Weston-super-Mare's Old Mixon factory.

During 1963 Westland was looking at Britain's future military helicopter requirements. This exercise produced several designs, one of which was to became the medium-sized multi-role WG.13, later named Lynx. Across the English Channel France was doing the same. The upshot was an Anglo-French agreement on collaborative production of the Lynx – for which Westland had responsibility – with the French Puma, a medium-sized transport helicopter, and Gazelle, a light five-seat communications and training type being built both by Westland and in France by Sud Aviation. These were to meet both countries' requirements. Although this did not materialise quite as planned, Westland built components for many of the French-built Pumas and also produced forty-eight complete Pumas for the RAF.

Westland's Lynx production grew into a major programme. The first aircraft flew in March 1971 and production, mostly for the Royal Navy, reached nearly 400 by 1997. The Lynx has been exported to twelve countries and, on 11 August 1986, became the first helicopter to set an over-400 kph world speed record, flying at 249.10 mph (400.87 kph) above the Somerset levels at Sedgemoor.

The Westland 30, a fifteen-seat civil helicopter, using the Lynx engine and transmission system, first flew in April 1979, two weeks ahead of schedule. But it was not to be a success. Only forty were built, small numbers being sold in the UK, USA and twenty-one in India, the last of these being grounded by 1990.

Westland however, was heading toward a decade of financial, legal and commercial trauma. In 1978 the company had entered into contracts for 250 Lynx with a group of Arab countries. They foundered when some countries withdrew their support, leaving Westland with estimated losses of £150 million. It was not until the early 1990s that compensation payments began to trickle through following legal battles in the Swiss courts. A more up-beat international agreement between Westland and the Italian Agusta company followed the MoD's go-ahead for development of Westland's WG.34 ASW helicopter to succeed the Sea King in RN service. As the Italian Navy wanted a similar aircraft, a joint company – European Helicopter Industries (EHI) – was formed by Westland and Agusta to produce and market this multi-role helicopter designated EH 101. This it has done very effectively.

With the prospect of diminishing helicopter production, in late 1983 Westland teamed with the Australian Aircraft Consortium to submit a turboprop contender, the A-20, as a Jet Provost successor for the RAF. In a four-cornered competition the A-20 lost to the Brazilian Embraer Tucano.

During 1984-86 Westland's problems were national headlines where they became 'the Westland Affair'. In essence, it was a vital financial restructuring of the company in which United Technologies in the USA and Fiat in Italy were to inject some £72 million into

Westland's first production anti-submarine Sea King 1, XV642, with a six-blade tail rotor and dorsal radome.

Westland. A licence to build and sell the Sikorsky Black Hawk helicopter and a guarantee of two million man-hours of work over a five-year period were part of the deal. The first order for eighty aircraft from Saudi Arabia was to have been placed in July 1988 – but it did not materialise. It was an affair which caused two Cabinet Ministers to resign and, in the longer run, may have affected the career of a Prime Minister.

While Sea King and Lynx production slowed, on 7 April 1987, the first Westland-built pre-production EH 101 was rolled out with its first flight taking place on 9 October. Seven weeks later Agusta's first EH 101 flew in Italy. Seven more pre-production prototypes were to follow them into the air. It was a good start to this joint production programme. Moreover, Westland's restructuring plan was working well and productivity was up some 15 per cent. Then, in 1988, Fiat decided that its shareholding in Westland didn't suit its plans for its future. GKN acquired the Italian company's shareholding plus some others to own 22.02 per cent of Westland.

In September 1991 the Ministry of Defence named a Westland/IBM consortium as prime contractor for EH 101 production. Three years later Westland became a wholly-owned GKN subsidiary. In the same year Team Apache brought together GKN Westland, McDonnell Douglas, Martin Marietta and Westinghouse to offer the Westland Apache attack helicopter (based on the US Army Longbow Apache) to meet British Army needs into the next century. In July 1995 the UK Government confirmed its choice of this helicopter for the Army Air Corps. The first of forty-four production EH 101s, designated Merlin HM1 for the Royal Navy, appeared in March 1996. Deliveries are scheduled from 1998 to 2001. A further twenty-two – the Merlin SH.3 – have been ordered for the RAF, the first being delivered on 25 November 1998. First orders have been placed for the civil Heliliner and the Italian Navy ordered a mixed bag of sixteen maritime, utility and airborne early warning variants.

As 1997 opened, plans were in hand for sixty-six WAH-64D Longbow Apaches to be delivered to the Army Air Corps between 2000-2003. In January 1998 Canada announced EH1 would get orders for fifteen EH101 SAR variants named 'Cormorant'.

GKN Westland marches toward the new millennium with confident and experienced steps, exhibiting again the spirit of the Petter twins who, as enthusiastic and patriotic volunteers, moved into the unknown-to-them aircraft manufacturing business and 'got on with it' more than eighty years ago.

A Sea King 1 on patrol along a rocky coastline in rough (ish) weather. The boat-shaped hull and sponsons were some comfort to the crew in the event of an emergency ditching.

Up from RNAS Culdrose, this anti-submarine Sea King 2 shows the main undercarriage retracted in the sponson and the icing and foreign object shield in front of the engine intakes.

A product of the 1982 Falklands War, the Sea King 2A airborne early warning variant was developed in eleven weeks. It carried a retractable Thorn EMI Searchwater radar scanner in an inflatable Kevlar dome. This aircraft served with 849 Squadron.

This splendid study of an RAF Sea King 3 with engines running and rotors turning, reveals many details of the aircraft's construction and layout.

An 846 Squadron Sea King 4 Commando in Norway in September 1985. It hefts a Volvo Bandvagn over-snow vehicle, weighing some 8,000 lb, attached to a low response beam to prevent it swinging and affecting the aircraft's handling.

Steady as she goes. The RAF's all-yellow search and rescue Sea King 3s are a familiar sight in Britain's coastal, moorland and mountain regions. Here the winch operator carefully hoists a crewman and stretchered casualty.

An 848 Squadron Sea King 4, ZG821, in the Saudi Arabian desert in January 1991 during the Gulf War. Note the covers on the engine air intakes and the pitot head.

The RN, Army Air Corps and RAF provided 22 Sea Kings, 19 Pumas, 23 Lynx and 23 Gazelles for Operation Granby. Westland met some 130 different requirements, compressing a year's work into five months. Here two Sea Kings stand ready for operations behind a tented support base in the desert.

'C'mon – let's get out of here!' The crewman in this Sea King 4 urges a marine commando platoon to hurry along into the aircraft during an exercise. All three helicopters have their engines running for a quick exit.

An 810 Squadron anti-submarine Sea King 6 (note flat topped radome) and the helicopter training ship RFA *Argus*. A casualty reception vessel in the Gulf War *Argus* took the first four Sea King 4s when it left Plymouth on 31 October 1990.

A German Navy Sea King 41 pictured during search and rescue trials in the English Channel.

Ubendum Wemendum: the 'Latinised' motto of all good Service Departments. This white and dayglo red Royal Norwegian Air Force Sea King 43 crashed in 1988 but was rebuilt by Westland and returned to service on 20 March 1989.

'Now – where does this pipe go?' Engineers checking over the Rolls-Royce Gnome turboshaft engines in a Sea King 50 for the Royal Australian Navy during 1974.

Looking very much like later production Lynx, this all-yellow first prototype is seen during its first flight at Yeovil on 21 March 1971. It was flown by Ron Gellatly, Westland's chief test pilot with Dave Gibbings, Flight Test Engineer.

The first utility variant development Lynx, XX153, in Army Air Corps camouflage paint scheme. Its skids differ from those on the first Lynx.

The sleek mock-up of the civil Westland 606 used the second Lynx airframe with a 2 ft 'plug' to lengthen the cabin. Launched in January 1975 at a helicopter seminar and exhibition in Disneyland, it attracted a lot of interest.

Plush seating and generous sized windows promised comfort for the Westland 606's twelve passengers. However, its high cost of ownership deterred customers and put a stopper on production plans.

Over England's green and pleasant land, en route to the 1976 Farnborough Air Display. From left to right: Lynx first prototype G-BEAD with Pratt & Whitney PT6-A engines, Lynx 2 XZ166 with four Sea Skua missiles, Lynx XX910, Lynx 1 with HOT missile pods.

An Army Air Corps Lynx attacks a ground target with Sura rocket projectiles. These were one of the wide variety of fixed and disposable armament which the Lynx could carry into battle.

Westland's 10,000lb all-up weight Ground Mobility Test Vehicle being operated by Peter Reid, its designer. It was a device to move skid-mounted Lynx helicopters under their own power. The wheeled undercarriage on the Lynx AH9 superceded it.

During the 1970s Westland produced several remotely piloted helicopters for battlefield surveillance/target acquisition. With two 20 hp engines, Wideye first flew in August 1978. All development was halted in about 1983.

Where Eagles Dare! The rigid rotor on the Lynx enabled the pilots of the Army Air Corps' display team – *The Eagles* – to present an amazing aerobatic programme including rolls and loops.

The 900 horsepower Rolls-Royce Gem turboshaft engines fit snugly into the Lynx's engine bays on top of the fuselage. Hinged cowling panels provide access to most of the engine and systems equipment.

With HMS *Gloucester* in the background this Lynx 2, XZ236, has been converted to represent an interim Lynx 8. It was used for central tactical system development.

Flight deck of a Lynx 3 of 700L Squadron, the Intensive Flying Trials Unit at RNAS Yeovilton, showing the central tactical system display.

Built in 1979 G-LYNX, the demonstrator aircraft was modified, updated and fitted with go-fast goodies for an attack on the helicopter world speed record. Its record speed of 400.87 km/h (249.10 mph), set on 11 August 1986, was the first to break the 400 km/h barrier.

ZD249, the first Lynx 3, was not the Super Lynx despite the name on the nose. It was reconfigured as an aerodynamic representation of the Lynx 8. Here it carries four British Aerospace Sea Skua anti-ship missiles.

Few recognised the first Lynx 1 modified and tweaked to become the Lynx 9 prototype. Mods included tricycle undercarriage, British Experimental Rotor Programme (BERP) rotor blades and jet-pipe diffusers to combat heat-seeking missiles.

The Lynx Three (not Lynx 3), ZE477, Westland's private venture Army helicopter designed to survive in a battlefield environment. Armoured and heavily armed with many advanced features and systems, it failed to win an order. This aircraft is in the International Helicopter Museum.

The first Lynx (FN)2 for the French Navy. It has the British serial XZ260 on the fin. Later the numerals were adopted as the French serial.

Brazilian Navy's Lynx 21. This is the fourth of nine aircraft originally ordered. It carries Westland's Class B registration G-17-14.

The first Lynx 99 for the Republic of Korea Navy which first flew on 16 November 1989. This was the launch order for Westland's new generation of naval Lynx.

Survival-suited passengers on a North Sea platform exit the first production Westland 30 Series 100, G-BIWY in British Airways Helicopters' livery.

During 1984 Omniflight Helicopters, acting on behalf of Pan American Airways, began scheduled Westland 30-100 services between John F. Kennedy International Airport and downtown New York. They ended on 1 February 1988.

'C'mon – let's get out of here!' – again. A Westland 30-100 lifts off having dropped a four-man mortar team during a demonstration of the aircraft in a military role.

The lone Westland 30-200 Series had two General Electric CT7-2B engines giving unrestricted single-engine capability at high ambient temperatures. The sideways-facing air intakes are noteworthy.

PP1 was the first of nine pre-production EH 101s. It is seen with Erecting Shop members on, or about, 7 April 1987 when it was officially rolled out with much pomp and circumstance plus a dry-ice and light show. Minister of Defence George Younger was the chief guest at this important event.

During 1986-87 Westland assembled Sikorsky-built components to produce this WS70 Black Hawk attack helicopter. It was expected that some 200 would be exported over a ten to fifteen year period. The plan never materialised.

'Up you come!' With a handful of collective pitch applied, Trevor Egginton, Westland chief test pilot, gets the EH 101 PP1 off the deck at Yeovil. Note the inverted aerofoil section of the tailplane.

Mock-up of the EH 101. The man gives scale to the giant main rotor head and the 1,600 shp General Electric T700-401 turboshaft engines, three of which powered early examples of this big helicopter.

This 'tail-on to the sun' view of PP3, the first civil EH 101, shows the arrowhead configuration of the three General Electric CT7-6 engines used in this variant.

The Westland-built EH 101 pre-production prototype PP4 with its air- and ground-crews and those involved with its first flight on 15 June 1989. From left to right: Roger Simonite, Allan Dougan, Garry Day, Roger Evans (crew chief), Ricky Jones (crew chief), Roland Starkey, Dave Marsh (flight test engineer), Dave Baker, Colin Hague (chief test pilot), Jerry Tracy (deputy chief test pilot), Barry Beaton (flight test engineer), Bill Carpenter, Dave Glover, Chris Tyler (chief flight test engineer), Andy Pearce, Nev Faulkner, Mark Hazzard, John Roe, Harry Ridgewell, Gilberto Tintori (Agusta flight test engineer), Marco Stuppi (Agusta).

Does its civil registration read 'Go 101' or 'G-Oi Oi'? It was certainly all go for Westland and this red, white and blue civil passenger-carrying Heliliner – EH 101 PP8 – when it appeared in the 1990 Farnborough Flying Display.

The Wonderful Wizard from Westland. EH 101 PP5, ZF649, the Royal Navy's Merlin anti-submarine helicopter, made its first deck landing on HMS *Norfolk* in November 1990. The 360 degree radome under the cabin is noteworthy.

The luxurious interior of the Heliliner. Its large windows, overhead lockers and comfortable seats for thirty passengers easily match those of the average fixed-wing regional airliner.

One of the four pre-production EH 101s built by Agusta SpA in Italy was the utility variant with a rear-loading ramp. It was originally scheduled to have 2,100 shp Rolls-Royce/Turbomeca/Piaggio RTM.322 turboshaft engines destined for use in production aircraft.

December 1992 with EH 101 PP5 undergoing deck trials in HMS *Iron Duke*. Here it is firmly secured to the rolling deck in a fairly choppy sea state. Aboard were Colin Hague and John Teasdale, pilot and co-pilot, with flight test engineers Dick Scrivener and Dave Marsh.

The three EH 101 variants fly together. From front to back: the Royal Navy's Merlin anti-submarine helicopter, the thirty-passenger civil Heliliner and the utility variant, which has a 'beanie' on its main rotor head to smooth airflow over the fin.

It takes less than two minutes for thirty combat-equipped troops to be loaded aboard the EH 101 utility variant via the rear ramp. Getting out again takes only forty seconds!

With its main rotor blades power-folded and the tail unit doubled up on itself, PP5 stands ready to be tucked away in HMS *Norfolk's* deck hangar. Like the Lysander – but for a different reason – EH 101 has a small aperture at the base of its fin. This one is for gear box cooling.

'Keep 'er coming'. Royal Navy engineers and aircrew watch carefully as the folded PP5 is inched into the deck hangar. This aircraft was dedicated to specific integration of Royal Navy weapons systems.

What appears to be a Heliliner heads this EH 101 production line at Yeovil. The first production Merlin HM1 for the Royal Navy was rolled out on 6 March 1996.

On 13 July 1995 the UK Government confirmed its choice of the Westland/McDonnell Douglas Helicopters WAH-64D Longbow Apache as the future all-weather attack helicopter for the Army Air Corps with a £2.5 billion order for sixty-six aircraft.

Westland's Battle Wagon. The Longbow Apache, armed with just about every guided and unguided weapon and sensing device known to man. Note the under-fuselage automatic 30 mm Chain Gun. The 'spare tyre' atop the rotorhead is a radome.

Acknowledgements

Shortly before this book was completed, the author and many hundreds of other people were saddened at the death of Harald Penrose. If any one man personified Westland it was Harald. He was with the company for more than four decades and had led the flight test team for almost all of his twenty-eight test flying years. He provided much of the detailed information and many of the photographs used in the book.

Keeping up-to-date with such a dynamic company as Westland is not easy. I am, therefore, most grateful to Christopher Loney, Director of Public Affairs – GKN Westland, who has provided details of his company's ongoing production programmes with photographs to match. I am also very much indebted to two ex-Westland stalwarts. Fred Ballam drew on his lifetime of service with the company in answering hundreds of searching questions; Peter Batten dug deep into photographic files to find long forgotten prints of Westland aeroplanes, people and events. Without their enthusiastic help over a number of years, neither this book nor my earlier one, *Westland Aircraft since 1915* in the Putnam Series, would have seen the light of day. I am grateful to Conway Maritime Publishing, publishers of that book, for their permission to produce this one. I am also much indebted to Martin Heal, the editor of the *Western Gazette* who enabled me to make contact with ex- and current Westland employees and their relations who have kindly lent me some of their precious photographs and provided some gems of information. They are Patricia Bird, J.F.Cornelius, Jane Daniels, Michael J. Evans, former Westland test pilot John Fay, Keith Griffiths, John Groves, Bob Gundry, Ron G.E. Hallett, Colin Hague, GKN-Westland Helicopters's chief test pilot, Janie Jacobs, Harry Ridgewell, Mike Taylor, Graham Toms and Clark Wyatt.

As always, my wife put the final polish on my PC-generated words, spell-checking and punctuating, to produce the final story ready for the publishers. My thanks also go to Alan Sutton, David Buxton and the staff of the Chalford Publishing Company for their continuing support with the creation of books such as this one.